CHRISTIAN SCIENCE

VERSUS

PANTHEISM

BY

MARY BAKER EDDY

PASTOR EMERITUS OF THE FIRST CHURCH OF CHRIST, SCIENTIST
BOSTON, AND AUTHOR OF SCIENCE AND HEALTH
WITH KEY TO THE SCRIPTURES

Registered
U. S. Patent Office

Published by The
Trustees under the Will of Mary Baker G. Eddy
BOSTON, U. S. A.

Authorized Literature of
THE FIRST CHURCH OF CHRIST, SCIENTIST
in Boston, Massachusetts

PRINTED IN THE UNITED STATES OF AMERICA

CHRISTIAN SCIENCE VERSUS PANTHEISM

PASTOR'S MESSAGE TO THE MOTHER
CHURCH, ON THE OCCASION OF THE
JUNE COMMUNION, 1898

SUBJECT: *Not Pantheism, but Christian Science.*

BELOVED brethren, since last you gathered at the
feast of our Passover, the winter winds have come
and gone; the rushing winds of March have shrieked and
hummed their hymns; the frown and smile of April, the
laugh of May, have fled; and the roseate blush of joyous
June is here and ours.

In unctuous unison with nature, mortals are hoping and
working, putting off outgrown, wornout, or soiled gar-
ments — the pleasures and pains of sensation and the
sackcloth of waiting — for the springtide of Soul. For
what a man seeth he hopeth not for, but hopeth for what
he hath not seen, and waiteth patiently the appearing
thereof. The night is far spent, and day is not distant in
the horizon of Truth — even the day when all people
shall know and acknowledge one God and one Christianity.

CHRISTIAN SCIENCE NOT PANTHEISM

At this period of enlightenment, a declaration from the pulpit that Christian Science is pantheism is anomalous to those who know whereof they speak — who know that Christian Science *is* Science, and therefore is neither hypothetical nor dogmatical, but demonstrable, and looms above the mists of pantheism higher than Mt. Ararat above the deluge.

ANALYSIS OF "PANTHEISM"

According to Webster the word "pantheism" is derived from two Greek words meaning "all" and "god." Webster's *derivation* of the English word "pantheism" is most suggestive. His uncapitalized word "god" gives the meaning of pantheism as a human opinion of "gods many," or mind in matter. "The doctrine that the universe, conceived of as a whole, is God; that there is no God but the combined forces and laws which are manifested in the existing universe."

The Standard Dictionary has it that pantheism is the doctrine of the deification of natural causes, conceived as one personified nature, to which the religious sentiment is directed.

Pan is a Greek prefix, but it might stand, in the term pantheism, for the mythological deity of that name; and *theism* for a belief concerning Deity in theology. However, Pan in imagery is preferable to pantheism in theology.

The mythical deity may please the fancy, while pantheism suits not at all the Christian sense of religion. Pan, as a deity, is supposed to preside over sylvan solitude, and is a horned and hoofed animal, half goat and half man, that poorly presents the poetical phase of the genii of forests.[1]

My sense of nature's rich glooms is, that loneness lacks but one charm to make it half divine — a friend, with whom to whisper, "Solitude is sweet." Certain moods of mind find an indefinable pleasure in stillness, soft, silent as the storm's sudden hush; for nature's stillness is voiced with a hum of harmony, the gentle murmur of early morn, the evening's closing vespers, and lyre of bird and brooklet.

> "O sacred solitude! divine retreat!
> Choice of the prudent! envy of the great!
> By thy pure stream, or in thy evening shade,
> We court fair wisdom, that celestial maid."

Theism is the belief in the personality and infinite mind of one supreme, holy, self-existent God, who reveals Himself supernaturally to His creation, and whose laws are not reckoned as science. In religion, it is a belief in one God, or in many gods. It is opposed to atheism and

[1] In Roman mythology (one of my girlhood studies), Pan stood for "universal nature proceeding from the divine Mind and providence, of which heaven, earth, sea, the eternal fire, are so many members." Pan was the god of shepherds and hunters, leader of the nymphs, president of the mountains, patron of country life, and guardian of flocks and herds. His pipe of seven reeds denotes the celestial harmony of the seven planets; his shepherd's crook, that care and providence by which he governs the universe; his spotted skin, the stars; his goat's feet, the solidity of the earth; his man-face, the celestial world.

1 monotheism, but agrees with certain forms of pantheism
and polytheism.   It is the doctrine that the universe owes
3 its origin and continuity to the reason, intellect, and will of
a self-existent divine Being, who possesses all wisdom,
goodness, and power, and is the creator and preserver of
6 man.

A theistic theological belief may agree with physics and
anatomy that reason and will are properly classified as
9 mind, located in the brain; also, that the functions of
these faculties depend on conditions of matter, or brain,
for their proper exercise.   But reason and will are human;
12 God is divine.   In academics and in religion it is patent
that will is capable of use and of abuse, of right and wrong
action, while God is incapable of evil; that brain is matter,
15 and that there are many so-called minds; that He is the
creator of man, but that man also is a creator, making
two creators; but God is Mind and one.

18   GOD — NOT HUMAN DEVICES — THE PRESERVER
OF MAN

God, Spirit, is indeed the preserver of man.   Then, in
21 the words of the Hebrew singer, "Why art thou cast down,
O my soul? and why art thou disquieted within me? hope
thou in God: for I shall yet praise Him, who is the health
24 of my countenance, and my God. . . . Who forgiveth
all thine iniquities; who healeth all thy diseases."   This
being the case, what need have we of drugs, hygiene, and
27 medical therapeutics, if these are not man's preservers?
By admitting self-evident affirmations and then contra-

dicting them, monotheism is lost and pantheism is found 1
in scholastic theology. Can a single quality of God,
Spirit, be discovered in matter? The Scriptures plainly 3
declare, "The Word was God;" and "all things were
made by Him," — the Word. What, then, can matter
create, or how can it exist? 6

Jesus' Definition of Evil

Did God create evil? or is evil self-existent, and so
possessed of the nature of God, good? Since evil is not 9
self-made, who or what hath made evil? Our Master
gave the proper answer for all time to this hoary query.
He said of evil: "Ye are of your father, the devil, and the 12
lusts of your father ye will do. He was a murderer from
the beginning, and abode not in the truth [God], because
there is no truth [reality] in him [evil]. When he speaketh 15
a lie, he speaketh of his own: for he is a liar, and the father
of it [a lie]."

Jesus' definition of devil (evil) explains evil. It shows 18
that evil is both liar and lie, a delusion and illusion. Therefore we should neither believe the lie, nor believe that it
hath embodiment or power; in other words, we should 21
not believe that a lie, nothing, can be something, but deny
it and prove its falsity. After this manner our Master cast
out evil, healed the sick, and saved sinners. Knowing 24
that evil is a lie, and, as the Scripture declares, brought
sin, sickness, and death into the world, Jesus treated the
lie summarily. He denied it, cast it out of mortal mind, 27
and thus healed sickness and sin. His treatment of evil

1 and disease, Science will restore and establish, — first,
because it was more effectual than all other means; and,
3 second, because evil and disease will never disappear in
any other way.

Finally, brethren, let us continue to denounce evil as the
6 illusive claim that God is not supreme, and continue to
fight it until it disappears, — but not as one that beateth
the mist, but lifteth his head above it and putteth his foot
9 upon a lie.

EVIL, AS PERSONIFIED BY THE SERPENT

Mosaic theism introduces evil, first, in the form of a
12 talking serpent, contradicting the word of God and thereby
obtaining social prestige, a large following, and changing
the order and harmony of God's creation. But the higher
15 criticism is not satisfied with this theism, and asks, If God
is *infinite* good, what and where is evil? And if Spirit
made all that was made, how can matter be an intelligent
18 creator or coworker with God? Again: Did one Mind,
or two minds, enter into the Scriptural allegory, in the
colloquy between good and evil, God and a serpent? — and
21 if two minds, what becomes of theism in Christianity? For
if God, good, is Mind, and evil also is mind, the Christian
religion has at least two Gods. If Spirit is sovereign, how
24 can matter be force or law; and if God, good, is omnipo-
tent, what power hath evil?

It is plain that elevating evil to the altitude of mind gives
27 it power, and that the belief in more than one spirit, if

Spirit, God, is infinite, breaketh the First Commandment
in the Decalogue.

Science shows that a plurality of minds, or intelligent
matter, signifies more than one God, and thus prevents the
demonstration that the healing Christ, Truth, gave and
gives in proof of the omnipotence of one divine, infinite
Principle.

Does not the theism or belief, that after God, Spirit, had
created all things spiritually, a material creation took
place, and God, the preserver of man, declared that man
should die, lose the character and sovereignty of Jehovah,
and hint the gods of paganism?

THEISTIC RELIGIONS

We know of but three theistic religions, the Mosaic, the
Christian, and the Mohammedan. Does not each of these
religions mystify the absolute oneness and infinity of God,
Spirit?

A close study of the Old and New Testaments in con-
nection with the original text indicates, in the third chap-
ter of Genesis, a lapse in the Mosaic religion, wherein
theism seems meaningless, or a vague apology for con-
tradictions. It certainly gives to matter and evil reality
and power, intelligence and law, which implies Mind,
Spirit, God; and the logical sequence of this error is idolatry — other gods.

Again: The hypothesis of mind in matter, or more than
one Mind, lapses into evil dominating good, matter govern-
ing Mind, and makes sin, disease, and death inevitable,

1 despite of Mind, or by the consent of Mind!   Next, it
follows that the disarrangement of matter causes a man to
3 be mentally deranged; and the Babylonian sun god, moon
god, and sin god find expression in sun worship, lunacy,
sin, and mortality.

6 Does not the belief that Jesus, the man of Galilee, is
God, imply two Gods, one the divine, infinite Person, the
other a human finite personality?   Does not the belief
9 that Mary was the mother of God deny the self-existence
of God?   and does not the doctrine that Mohammed is
the only prophet of God infringe the sacredness of one
12 Christ Jesus?

Scientific Christianity Means One God

Christianity, as taught and demonstrated in the first
15 century by our great Master, virtually annulled the so-
called laws of matter, idolatry, pantheism, and polytheism.
Christianity then had one God and one law, namely,
18 divine Science.   It said, "Call no man your father upon
the earth, for one is your Father, which is in heaven."
Speaking of himself, Jesus said, "My Father is greater
21 than I."   Christianity, as he taught and demonstrated it,
must ever rest on the basis of the First Commandment and
love for man.

24 The doctrines that embrace pantheism, polytheism, and
paganism are admixtures of matter and Spirit, truth and
error, sickness and sin, life and death.   They make man
27 the servant of matter, living by reason of it, suffering because of it, and dying in consequence of it.   They con-

stantly reiterate the belief of pantheism, that mind "sleeps in the mineral, dreams in the animal, and wakes in man."

"Infinite Spirit" means one God and His creation, and no reality in aught else. The term "spirits" means more than one Spirit; — in paganism they stand for gods; in spiritualism they imply men and women; and in Christianity they signify a good Spirit and an evil spirit.

Is there a religion under the sun that hath demonstrated one God and the four first rules pertaining thereto, namely, "Thou shalt have no other gods before me;" "Love thy neighbor as thyself;" "Be ye therefore perfect, even as your Father which is in heaven is perfect;" "Whosoever liveth and believeth in me shall never die." (John xi. 26.)

What mortal to-day is wise enough to do himself no harm, to hinder not the attainment of scientific Christianity? Whoever demonstrates the highest humanity, — long-suffering, self-surrender, and spiritual endeavor to bless others, — ought to be aided, not hindered, in his holy mission. I would kiss the feet of such a messenger, for to help such a one is to help one's self. The demonstration of Christianity blesses all mankind. It loves one's neighbor as one's self; it loves its enemies — and this love benefits its enemies (though they believe it not), and rewards its possessor; for, "If ye love them which love you, what reward have ye?"

MAN THE TRUE IMAGE OF GOD

From a material standpoint, the best of people sometimes object to the philosophy of Christian Science, on the ground that it takes away man's personality and makes man less than man. But what saith the apostle? — even this: "If a man think himself to be something, when he is nothing, he deceiveth himself." The great Nazarene Prophet said, "By their fruits ye shall know them:" then, if the effects of Christian Science on the lives of men be thus judged, we are sure the honest verdict of humanity will attest its uplifting power, and prevail over the opposite notion that Christian Science lessens man's individuality.

The students at the Massachusetts Metaphysical College, generally, were the average man and woman. But after graduation, the best students in the class averred that they were stronger and better than before it. With twelve lessons or less, the present and future of those students had wonderfully broadened and brightened before them, thus proving the utility of what they had been taught. Christian Scientists heal functional, organic, chronic, and acute diseases that M.D.'s have failed to heal; and, better still, they reform desperate cases of intemperance, tobacco using, and immorality, which, we regret to say, other religious teachers are unable to effect. All this is accomplished by the grace of God, — the effect of God *understood*. A higher manhood is manifest, and never lost, in that individual who finds the highest joy, — therefore no pleasure in loathsome habits or in sin, and no necessity for disease and death. Whatever promotes statuesque being, health, and holiness does not degrade man's personality. Sin, sickness, appetites, and passions, constitute no part of man, but obscure man. Therefore it

required the divinity of our Master to perceive the real
man, and to cast out the unreal or counterfeit. It caused
St. Paul to write, — "Lie not one to another, seeing that
ye have put off the old man with his deeds; and have put
on the new man, which is renewed in knowledge after
the image of Him that created him."

Was our Master mistaken in judging a cause by its
effects? Shall the opinions, systems, doctrines, and dog-
mas of men gauge the animus of man? or shall his stature
in Christ, Truth, declare him? Governed by the divine
Principle of his being, man is perfect. When will the
schools allow mortals to turn from clay to Soul for the
model? The Science of being, understood and obeyed,
will demonstrate man to be superior to the best church-
member or moralist on earth, who understands not this
Science. If man is spiritually fallen, it matters not what
he believes; he is not upright, and must regain his native
spiritual stature in order to be in proper shape, as certainly
as the man who falls physically needs to rise again.

Mortals, content with something less than perfection —
the original standard of man — may believe that evil de-
velops good, and that whatever strips off evil's disguise be-
littles man's personality. But God enables us to know that
evil is not the medium of good, and that good supreme de-
stroys all sense of evil, obliterates the lost image that
mortals are content to call man, and demands man's un-
fallen spiritual perfectibility.

The grand realism that man is the true image of God,
not fallen or inverted, is demonstrated by Christian Science.
And because Christ's dear demand, "Be ye therefore

1 perfect," is valid, it will be found possible to fulfil it. Then
also will it be learned that good is not educed from evil,
3 but comes from the rejection of evil and its *modus operandi*.
Our scholarly expositor of the Scriptures, Lyman Abbott,
D.D., writes, "God, Spirit, is ever in universal nature."
6 Then, we naturally ask, how can Spirit be constantly pass-
ing out of mankind by death — for the universe includes
man?

9 ## THE GRANDEUR OF CHRISTIANITY

This closing century, and its successors, will make strong
claims on religion, and demand that the inspired Scriptural
12 commands be fulfilled. The altitude of Christianity open-
eth, high above the so-called laws of matter, a door that no
man can shut; it showeth to all peoples the way of escape
15 from sin, disease, and death; it lifteth the burden of sharp
experience from off the heart of humanity, and so lighteth
the path that he who entereth it may run and not weary,
18 and walk, not wait by the roadside, — yea, pass gently on
without the alterative agonies whereby the way-seeker
gains and points the path.
21 The Science of Christianity is strictly monotheism, —
it has ONE GOD. And this divine infinite Principle,
noumenon and phenomena, is demonstrably the self-
24 existent Life, Truth, Love, substance, Spirit, Mind, which
includes all that the term implies, and is all that is real and
eternal. Christian Science is irrevocable — unpierced
27 by bold conjecture's sharp point, by bald philosophy, or
by man's inventions. It is divinely true, and every hour

in time and in eternity will witness more steadfastly to its   1
practical truth.   And Science is not pantheism, but Christian Science.   3

Chief among the questions herein, and nearest my
heart, is this: When shall Christianity be demonstrated
according to Christ, in these words: "Neither shall they   6
say, Lo, here! or, lo there! for, behold, the kingdom of
God is within you"?

EXHORTATION   9

Beloved brethren, the love of our loving Lord was never
more manifest than in its stern condemnation of all error,
wherever found.   I counsel thee, rebuke and exhort one   12
another.   Love all Christian churches for the gospel's
sake; and be exceedingly glad that the churches are united
in purpose, if not in method, to close the war between   15
flesh and Spirit, and to fight the good fight till God's will
be witnessed and done on earth as in heaven.

Sooner or later all shall know Him, recognize the great   18
truth that Spirit is infinite, and find life in Him in whom
we do "live, and move, and have our being" — life in
Life, all in All.   Then shall all nations, peoples, and   21
tongues, in the words of St. Paul, have "one God and
Father of all, who is above all, and through all, and in
you all."   (Ephesians iv. 6.)   24

Have I wearied you with the mysticism of opposites?
Truly there is no rest in them, and I have only traversed
my subject that you may prove for yourselves the unsub-   27

stantial nature of whatever is unlike good, weigh a sigh, and rise into the rest of righteousness with its triumphant train.

Once more I write, Set your affections on things above; love one another; commune at the table of our Lord in one spirit; worship in spirit and in truth; and if daily adoring, imploring, and living the divine Life, Truth, Love, thou shalt partake of the bread that cometh down from heaven, drink of the cup of salvation, and be baptized in Spirit.

PRAYER FOR COUNTRY AND CHURCH

Pray for the prosperity of our country, and for her victory under arms; that justice, mercy, and peace continue to characterize her government, and that they shall rule all nations. Pray that the divine presence may still guide and bless our chief magistrate, those associated with his executive trust, and our national judiciary; give to our congress wisdom, and uphold our nation with the right arm of His righteousness.

In your peaceful homes remember our brave soldiers, whether in camp or in battle.[1] Oh, may their love of country, and their faithful service thereof, be unto them life-preservers! May the divine Love succor and protect them, as at Manila, where brave men, led by the dauntless Dewey, and shielded by the power that saved them, sailed victoriously through the jaws of death and blotted out the Spanish squadron.

Great occasion have we to rejoice that our nation, which

[1] This refers to the war between United States and Spain for the liberty of Cuba.

fed her starving foe, — already murdering her peaceful
seamen and destroying millions of her money, — will be
as formidable in war as she has been compassionate in
peace.

May our Father-Mother God, who in times past hath
spread for us a table in the wilderness and "in the midst
of our enemies," establish us in the most holy faith, plant
our feet firmly on Truth, the rock of Christ, the "substance
of things hoped for" — and fill us with the life and under-
standing of God, and good will towards men.

MARY BAKER EDDY

MESSAGE

TO

THE MOTHER CHURCH

BOSTON, MASS.

JUNE, 1900